The Window

The Window
Tarik Kiswanson

JBE Books

DELIVERY

The title is important. The poem is not the one who dies. You can order the book. Through the window of my bedroom.

I speak from myself to myself. At this hour, I read myself and I hear myself simultaneously. I make myself hollow. I fill and empty myself. I pour myself. It's beyond what I need.

I find myself moving again, being profoundly moved by the fact that everything is out of control. I can feel the trembling. I can feel the instability. I shiver.

In the mayhem of our lives I remember the past. My one and many. At first I couldn't, but upon reflection I'm taken back to the summer of 1995. An image of a raw landscape appeared, taking me back to where it all started. To the foreign countryside that made me, from the violent and wet winds of the North Sea to the dead roots gone dry in an arid desert.

A glass shattered.

I am taken back to all my different beginnings.

FOR THE SAKE OF MEMORY

To see or not to see.

To look down and read without seeing.

To be without eyes.

To hear without your eyes.

To touch without feeling.

To touch for the first time,
and immediately last time.

To believe or not believe.

And in your mind.

And the home you made
and never lived in.

And the home you made
and never slept in.

And the weight of your body,
and the weight of mine.

And the moment your voice changed,
and the moment mine did.

And the heat only to immediately
be thrown in the cold.

And the cells dividing
while you are thinking.

And the cells surviving
when your spirit is missing.

And the body you nurture.

And the body you destroy.

To spread your fingers out for the first,
and immediately last time.

And the hours of disbelief.

And then the hours of belief.

And then all the things that they don’t see
but you feel.

Afraid of dying
and then of living.

Afraid of believing
and then belonging.

To remember only to forget.

A switch of language briefly appears, changing
the entire meaning of the sentence.

Transforming you.

NEW WORD

A new word appears, and the world is changed forever.

A new word sinks into you. Lingers within you. Becomes part of you. As you read, language takes hold of you.

A word that stays with you.
Sounds that never left you.
Endlessly transforming you.

In the sharpness and roundness, you are born anew.

Words disappearing inside of you. In the abyss of your mind, words and sentences, echoes of memories move through you.

Opposite the window.

THE WINDOW

Through the mirror opposite my window I see everything I need.

I leave all doors open. I close my eyes and forget the hours. As the ear is silenced by the night, the world goes numb. Night has no time.

I go in and out of consciousness. I enter and exit my apartment relentlessly. I make myself transparent. Light hits and I become the mirror. I absorb and I reflect.

In dreams, I find myself astray. I tremble. I panic. I feel full. I feel empty. I feel a great deal of relief. I can leave and come back infinitely. In my bedroom, I can come and go as I please.

I choose to doubt, I leave behind the certitude of everything.

O

The world as reflections in a mirror. The world as the vitreous body of the eye.

At the creation of O, we dream to enter it.

Mirror.

Its surface reminds us that the world is ever present, nothing disappears in our absence; the world never ceased to exist even when you were looking in the other direction.

WORDLESS

Between the reflections I move.

I enter and exit many rooms. Now, as I move, there is no looking back. The past is far behind, inside of me, and the future still, always, outside of me. Here, from myself to myself, I look inwards. Here, from myself to myself, I look into my eyes.

There is no reason. For all the reasons. Better let go of than hold onto.

Holding and keeping, words come to me. Holding and keeping, words are leaving me. Hold and keep, stay close to me. Remember me. Now, as night falls, move separately.

Look further, move beyond, he told me. I said, he says, looking at me; stay in between.

As I enter and exit many rooms, now at this moment, as I enter and exit, words keep coming to me.

If the word is used, it will survive.

CORRESPONDENCE

There is a book being written, there is a writer writing. By myself, within myself, I am in transit.

The book is not physical. Not something that can be held or observed. The book is a place. Suspended beneath us, levitating above us. Others will read. Others will often visit.

The book is a body. We are breathing at the same rhythm, moving to the same sound at the same speed.

The book is a park. There are countless entries and exits. Know your hours, know your days. Now your hours, now your days.

The book is a club. Like all pages, we are intimately close to each other. Words touching words.

The book is a corporate building. Endless glass windows, all of them are open. Between belief and disbelief we live.

The book will have a title. A title will emerge. A new title will surface. Something new, someone new, the readers will always keep reading.

The book will travel. The book will be forgotten. Some things, most things, will most definitely be forgotten.

Through more pages I read.

SUBURB OF SILENCE

No longer is the writer writing what he imagines, but what he remembers.

As the window expands, familiar sounds surround me.

Suddenly silence pervades.

I am walking backwards. To where it all started.
The voice of my brother. Through the suburb of silence.

As the hour is late, I hear him call.

We move, moved each other, transformed one another in the suburb of silence. Disappearing in the crowd, for years he whispered in the ear of silence.

Displaced from places we couldn't be, we were linked by something no one could see.

I move closer.

DRIFT

I get close, closer. I become the mirror. I am unrecognizable. I stare and stick to its shiny surface. I absorb and get absorbed. I shift in size and shape.

I am relentlessly pulled out of myself and thrown back into myself. I am tall. I am thin. I am lost.

The world shakes and all shatters. Bare feet and glass crackles. Memory door left open, phone vibrates, all lines open.

The silence is given word. She reasons with me and I give ear. She moves from building to building from body to body. Blinded by the night I drift.

Blurry borders and light. Blurry body in the night.

Half awake half asleep.

Blurry borders in the night. Blurry body through the light.

CORRESPONDENCE II

I am left at the entrance. On the threshold of consciousness. So many things so suddenly unavailable to my mind. Winds hit hard and grey clouds surround me.

In the absence of sun, I manage to find heat in the cold. I let myself feel more, be more. Heavy breaths, bits and pieces shattered and scattered.

A friend writes and I reply:

In the palm of my hand, your warmth has reached me.

Though in the wait, fear not my forgetfulness. Our breaths are synchronized, our hearts beat at the same speed to the same rhythm through the same night. Shatter the norm, shatter yourself, become more in the O.

All doors are open.

Let's fall faster.

Let's fall faster.

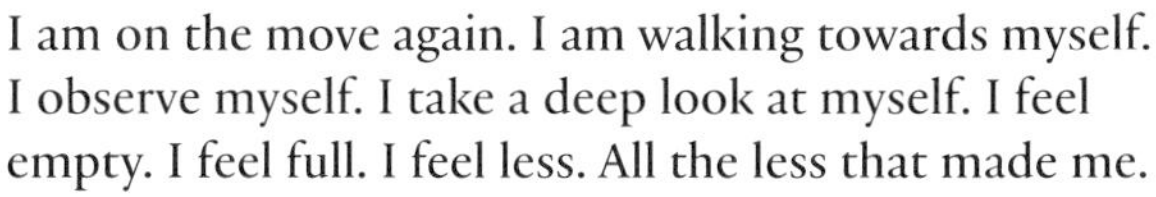
I am on the move again. I am walking towards myself. I observe myself. I take a deep look at myself. I feel empty. I feel full. I feel less. All the less that made me.

rootless,

wireless,

horizonless,

comfortless,

weightless,

roadless,

traditionless,

homeless,

needless,

l - e - s - s

To want to be less. To be better being less. To always be more by being less. To feel more than I could bear. To be more than I could bear.

Take me back to the book.

SPACES

The spaces in between are not empty. There is no
silence.

I observe. I turn around. I stretch my body.
With my eyes between all words I lift my body.

I fill up all spaces. With my whole body.

I divide myself, my body.

In the spaces between the words –
transparent to the eye, transparent body.

Endless space and my body.

I turn again.

There is no silence.

What is not read with the eye, not heard by the ear.

All the things I do with my body.

Sleepless.

THE DREAM

Detectives continue their way through the dusty dining hall and the word is out.

He went to sleep earlier than expected. Radiators heating his fragile house as the numb parts are shifting position in the hours of sleep. I believe, he believes, we are in the house of sleep.

Fallen into a space of rest, he mumbles a monologue no one can perceive. Between what he sees and what he knows, he has now abandoned all belief.

A home with no doors or windows, all he sees is the rest he needs.

Shivers run up and down his stairs. No one can resist, your body has entered the house of sleep.

The house shakes.

His bones ache.

This is the house of sleep.

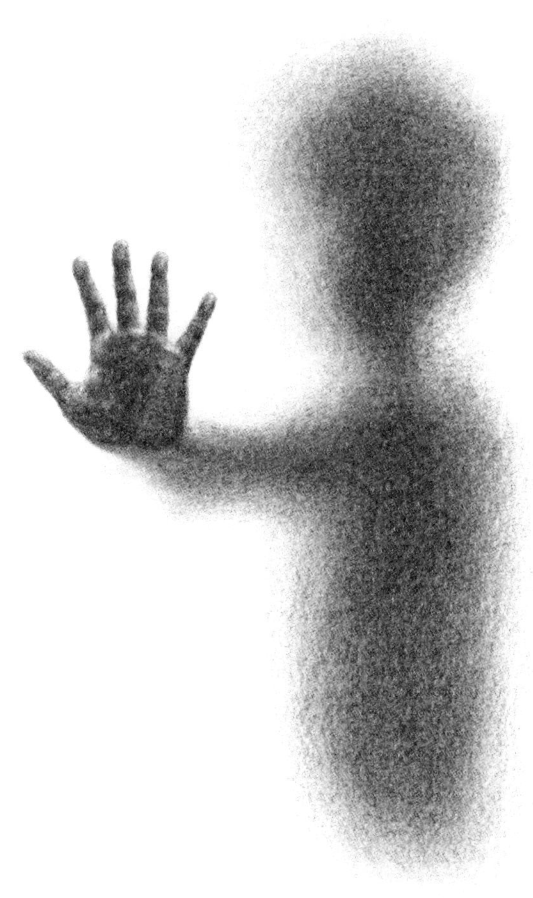

Tarik Kiswanson is a poet and an artist. He was born in 1986 in Halmstad, Sweden, where his parents exiled from Palestine and Jordan in the early 1980s. His work encompasses sculpture, writing, performance, drawing, sound and video works. Notions of rootlessness, regeneration, and renewal are central themes in his oeuvre. His practice evinces an engagement with the poetics of métissage: a means of writing and surviving between multiple conditions and contexts. His various bodies of work can be understood as a cosmology of related conceptual families, each exploring variations on themes like refraction, multiplication, disintegration, levitation, hybridity, and polyphony through their own distinct language.

Previous spread: Tarik Kiswanson, *The Window*, 2020, charcoal drawing, 42 × 29,7 cm © Tarik Kiswanson and Carré d'Art – Musée d'Art Contemporain

Direction
Mathieu Cénac and David Desrimais
Assisted by Juliette Chambon

Editor
Jesi Khadivi

Graphic Design
Montasser Drissi

Typefaces
Antique Legacy
Practice

Paper
Multidesign Natural

This publication is made possible with the support of the Museum van Hedendaagse Kunst Antwerpen in Belgium.

ISBN: 978-2-36568-051-6
Legal deposit: May 2022
Printed in Lithuania

JBE Books
90 rue de la Folie Méricourt
75011 Paris
jbe-books.com